Time Management
Is An
Oxymoron

Time Management Is An Oxymoron

Learn how to get more done in less time!

An entertaining guide to managing paper, e-mail,
the telephone, people and yourself effectively

By
MAYNARD ROLSTON

plus
DON HUTSON

ISBN: 1-58597-096-4

Library of Congress Control Number: 2001132072

A division of Squire Publishers, Inc.
4500 College Blvd.
Leawood, KS 66211
1/888/888-7696
www.leatherspublishing.com

TABLE OF CONTENTS

ACKNOWLEDGMENTS

The reason I titled this book "Time Management is an Oxymoron" is because you cannot manage time.

I started writing this book three years ago, and the first version was written in text book form. My friend, Rose Von Behren, was the first reader and made several suggestions. We didn't speak for three days, but she was right as it was poorly written.

While recovering from knee replacement, I rewrote the book, as she suggested, in story form. The book now made much more sense. To bring the material from a transcript to book form, I needed assistance from Brent Scholz.

Don Hutson and Chris Crouch were excellent advisors in the additional editing of this book. My good friend, Charles Stanley, has been a great coach over the years by giving my reports and book transcript "Charlie edits."

I looked for months for a publisher that I felt I could trust and who could help a novice like me get a book published. Fortunately, I found Tom Leathers who, along with his staff, helped make a dream come true. I also want to thank Leslie Eden, Sharen Lucero, Les Meredith, Mike Upchurch and Joe and Kim Rolston for their suggestions.

To our readers, I hope you will get as much pleasure out of reading this book as I did in writing it.

FOREWORD

Several years ago, I was seriously debating what to do about a huge problem. I worked for a Fortune 500 company and I was given a corporate-wide assignment to help stop the "paper handling madness." At that time, we had over 12,000 employees and the flood of memos, reports, and various other paper documents was getting out of hand. This flood of paper was increasing stress, increasing anxiety and significantly decreasing productivity among our employees. I read books and listened to tapes on the topic. I tried this technique and that technique. Some ideas were good; some were ridiculous. Nothing I read, heard or tried struck me as "the perfect solution" to the paper-handling problem.

Then I called my friend Don Hutson who has been involved in training for over thirty years and told him of my dilemma. Without hesitation he said, "Call my friend Maynard Rolston. If it has to do with managing paper, *he's the best.*"

I called Maynard, *It was a life-changing phone call.*

We chatted a few minutes. He said some things that sounded interesting so I decided to hire him to come in and show me his process. I didn't really expect much but it was my job to keep trying until I solved the problem.

Before I met Maynard, I was no slouch at maintaining an organized work space and an organized life. I was given the assignment because I was thought of as one of the most organized people in the company. I really didn't expect Maynard to teach me a lot about being organized. I was wrong! His system literally astounded me. I couldn't believe the elegance and simplicity of his system. I am passionate about learning processes that can help me get more done with less effort. I am fascinated with techniques that help me gain and maintain control over my life. About one hour into my training session with Maynard, I knew I had found what I was looking for.

Maynard's system helps us re-gain control over our workdays, improve concentration, enhance our focus on priorities, delegate more effectively, follow-up on assignments better, recover from unexpected interruptions quicker, coordinate with co-workers more effectively and, ultimately it will make life easier and less hectic. It is a high impact, low maintenance process. His ideas on e-mail, telephone, delegation, meetings and self-management are excellent. Learn to use his system and begin enjoying the benefits *that* day.

If you enjoy chaos, stress, anxiety and low productivity, don't bother reading this book. But, if you are ready to end these things once and for all, here and now, read on.

If you read this book, you are drawing on the knowledge and experience of a true master at what he does. Read this book, and implement his ideas and you will know what it feels like to be back in control of your life. I will always be grateful for the wisdom Maynard has shared with me. You made a wise decision when you got a copy of this book. Read about his system, but, more importantly, implement it as soon as possible and you will be much more efficient.

Chris Crouch
Co-author, *The Contented Achiever and Simple Works*

INTRODUCTION

Why are increasing numbers of employees not getting their work completed within a reasonable amount of time? Why are more managers spending long hours in the office, less time at home and are experiencing increased stress and burn out?

I believe that today's managers and employees need to be better organized in order to succeed in the workplace. The problem started in the '80s, when salaries increased too fast and climbed too high.

In the '90s, company executives realized that employee costs were too high and reacted by reducing the number of employees. Then, in the late '90s everyone seemed to be downsizing. Guess what didn't decrease, the work load! In addition to more paperwork, voice mail and e-mail traffic increased tremendously. Employees that may have performed adequately in the '80s and early '90s were now having a difficult time getting all their work done. Today, employees must know how to manage multiple tasks and get more work done in less time.

I can help!

After graduating from Oklahoma State University with a degree in Business and serving three years as an officer in the Air Force, I was employed by an oil company in Kansas City, Missouri.

Because of my data processing experience in the Air Force, I was selected to learn computer programming. After assisting in the implementation and operation of my employer's computer system, I went to work for a large manufacturer as the assistant manager of data processing. During these years, I wrote many computer programs and helped set up five computer systems.

After ten years, I decided to leave the computer field. I was offered an administrative assistant position for a vice president, responsible for about 70% of the company's sales.

My new boss was the most organized person I had ever known. I was amazed at how much work he could do while still maintaining a clean desk. Fortunately, he was the type of person who required his staff to adapt his efficient methods. During this time, my knowledge of how to manage paperwork improved dramatically.

For the next several years, I managed operations using effective paper managing techniques and found operating from a clean desk much more productive.

Then, the company reorganized, my boss retired and the job was no longer enjoyable. I started dreading Sunday evenings because Monday morning was not far away. Once again, the search for a new career began.

In 1981, I decided to go into business for myself, as a management consultant working with companies on improving profits.

After working with several types of organizations, I found most had one thing in common, the managers and employees didn't know how to manage paperwork effectively.

In July 1984, a magazine article was published about my paper managing techniques and people started calling me. Over the next several years, I worked with individuals, conducted workshops for companies and spoke at conventions teaching many people how to get more work done in less time.

The last chapter in this book is by Don Hutson. I first met Don as a client in the early '80s, and we later became friends. He is one of the finest sales trainers in the United States. Several years ago we implemented the paper managing process, which improved his productivity immensely. I know you'll benefit from his comments.

All the events in this book are based on actual experiences with real people in organizations throughout the United States. These included all types of companies, government agencies, schools and not-for-profit organizations.

The most difficult part of the program is committing to improve your productivity.

Although this book is written about a mythical director named John, please consider all the issues we cover no matter where you are in your career. Many of the issues we discuss will apply to you now and in the future.

This book covers more than how to manage paper. It covers e-mail, the telephone, management techniques and how to better manage yourself. When you implement the ideas presented in this book, you will get more work done in less time, with less stress, forever!

CHAPTER 1

Why You Need to Be Better Organized and Symptoms of Disorganization

THE PHONE was ringing when I entered my office. I answered, "Good morning, this is Maynard Rolston."

"This is John Jacobs. Are you the guy that helps people manage paperwork effectively?" the caller asked.

"I am indeed 'the guy;' what can I do for you?"

Over the last several years, I have received numerous calls just like John's. He asked if he could set up an appointment with me to see if I could help him.

I began by asking him what the top of his work area looked like. His reply was that it was covered with paper. I could tell just by the tone of his voice that he had just about had it with his job. We set up an appointment to meet in two weeks.

As usual, I arrived early. I've made it a habit, when going to a location where I've never been, to allow myself extra travel time. I would rather be twenty minutes early than one minute late.

I was cheerfully greeted by John's assistant, Joyce and she escorted me into his office.

Upon entering his office, I saw that his desk was piled high with paper and that his office was very cluttered. There were stacks of file folders, magazines and loose papers everywhere. There were so many stacks, you couldn't even tell what the top of his desk looked like. His credenza was also completely covered with paper. John had a worried look on his face and I could tell he wanted to do something immediately.

We shook hands. I then sat down in front of his desk and said, "John, tell me about your job and how long you've been doing it."

"I'm a director," he said, "and my staff is responsible for supporting the sales side of our company. I have six people reporting directly to me and a total of sixty people working for me. I've been with the company fifteen years, and in this job for three of those years; quite frankly, I think I'm just about burned out."

"Overall," I asked, "what is the biggest problem for your area?"

"Getting my work done on time," he quickly replied.

"I see that your desk is quite cluttered," I said. "Is this normal?"

"Yes," John said, "I periodically clear it off but in just a short period of time the paper is back on top of the desk."

"Does this cluttered desk hurt your concentration?" I asked.

John replied, "Yes, it also bothers me that I have to keep going back and forth between stacks."

"Do you have trouble finding files?" I asked.

"Oh yeah, all the time," he replied. "And the longer I look for a file, the more frustrated I get."

> *The average person spends about 150 hours per year looking for things in their own office. I sensed this figure was higher for John.*

"John" I asked, "how many hours a week are you in the office?"

John paused for about a minute. I could tell he was calculating in his mind how many hours he spent.

"About seventy hours per week," he answered. "And I also take work home. The thing that upsets me the most is I don't have enough time to do things for myself and my family."

"How much work do you feel you're getting done?" I asked.

He paused again, "Probably about thirty-five hours."

I then said, "If you divide the number of hours of work you feel you're getting done by the number of hours you're at work, you'll come up with a percentage figure that I call the

Employee Productivity Index.

> *Hours of productive work divided by total hours worked equals the Employee Productivity Index (EPI).*

> *In John's case, dividing thirty-five by seventy equals an EPI of 50%.*

I continued, "Over the years, I have found that thousands of employees have an EPI of 50% or less. In other words, if a person spends fifty hours a week working on their job, with a 50% EPI, they're getting only twenty-five hours of actual work done."

John asked, "Where do the other twenty-five hours go?"

"Good question," I replied. "Based on experience, I've discovered that they go to such nonproductive activities as:

1. Working on the wrong things.
2. Using the telephone ineffectively.
3. Using e-mail ineffectively.
4. Attending unorganized or unnecessary meetings.
5. Allowing people to pop-in unannounced.
6. Managing their own schedule inefficiently.
7. Following-up inconsistently.
8. Delegating ineffectively.
9. Scheduling work ineffectively.
10. Scheduling travel plans ineffectively.
11. Taking other people's problems.
12. Excessive visiting with other employees.

13. Making several trips to the copier, fax machine or file cabinet with only one item per trip.
14. Fretting over the piles of paper in their work area and what needs to be done."

"These are most of the things that waste people's time and adversely affect their productivity. But, don't worry, we'll cover all these items."

John asked, "What should my percentage of productivity be?"

I replied, "I think your EPI should be between 70% and 80%. This means, if you can raise your EPI to 80%, you'll not only reduce the time you're working by twenty hours, but you'll also get more work done, in less time."

I show managers, like John, how to manage from a clean desk. When you learn how to do so, the following happens:

1. Your distractions decrease.
2. Your concentration increases.
3. Your productivity increases.
4. Your level of anxiety decreases.
5. Your EPI increases.

I continued, "Today, almost everyone needs to be better organized because of what has happened in the work place. I believe that in the '80s, salaries increased too quickly and went too high. In the early '90s, company executives realized that employee costs were too high and reacted by reducing the number of employees. Downsizing was happening all over, even though work loads were increasing.

"There are far more distractions than ever. For example, look at the number of e-mails and voice mails employees receive per day. Employees who could function just fine in the '80s are having a difficult time completing their work. It's imperative that employees learn how to get more done in less time.

"One way to get more work done, is by eliminating tasks that are not worth the time. In the twenty-first century, we simply must be better organized and more efficient."

John got a funny look on his face and said, "That is exactly what happened here. I'm trying to do the same amount of work, but with fewer people."

I replied, "Should you hire me, John I want you to know that I'm an implementing consultant, and we will implement the process while I'm here. Together, we'll set up a program that will work for you. For most clients, this approach results in considerable productivity improvement, forever!

"John, there are two things we cannot change: twenty-four hours in a day and seven days in a week. However, there are three things we can change: your paper, e-mail and telephone managing habits; your management techniques; and your self-management skills.

"When you're not getting all your work done, you have only two choices: Work longer hours or figure out how to get more done in less time. If you're willing, I can show you how to do the latter."

John asked if he was the most disorganized person I'd ever seen.

"Absolutely not!" I replied. "The most disorganized person I ever worked with had piles of paper everywhere; on his desk, his credenza, on the floor, and even under his desk. It took us two full days to get his office cleared and the program implemented. However, before we could make any progress, I had to convince him that his clutter was adversely affecting his career. Years later, I learned this individual had become a highly respected vice president."

I then gave John a piece of sage advice: "Change takes place when the pain not to change exceeds the pain to change."

I could see a light bulb come on in John's head.

"What a great statement!" he exclaimed. "I'm going to write it down so I'll remember it in the future."

I then asked, "John, you told me that you have six people reporting directly to you. Are any of the six spending seventy hours per week in the office?"

"No," he answered.

I then asked, "Who sold you on that program?"

John hired me that day, and we scheduled a time for our

work to begin.

I insisted that he not schedule any meetings during our session and that he have three packages of hanging file folders with the small tabs (1/5" cut) available for our session. I also requested that he not clean up his office before my scheduled visit.

I could tell he felt better immediately. Just the anticipation of improving his situation improved his frame of mind. We shook hands again and I left.

CHAPTER 2

Learning the Five Action Decisions on What to Do with Paper and E-Mail

I ARRIVED EARLY at John's office and was greeted by Joyce. I had visited with her earlier, and assured her that her assistance was needed in making John more productive.

In my experience, I've found that executive assistants are among the most under utilized people in large corporations.

John arrived shortly after I did, and we went into his office. I sat in front of his desk, still piled high with paper.

"Does all this paper on your desk still bother you?" I asked.

"It depresses me," John said. "I get up in the morning in a great mood; I drive to the office listen to good music and then walk into my office, look at this pile on top of my desk, and get depressed. I hate Sunday evenings, because that means Monday morning is not far away."

I asked, "Have you heard time management experts advise you to 'handle each piece of paper one time'?" He nodded affirmatively.

"Well, they don't know what they're talking about," I told him. "In your job there is no way you can handle each piece of paper just one time."

John broke into a big smile and said "I've been trying to do that for months, unsuccessfully, and thought there was something wrong with me."

"John," I said, "There is nothing wrong with you; their concept is wrong.

"I am different from most management consultants in two ways: first, I have had more than twenty years of management experience, so believe me when I say I know what goes on behind your desk, and, second, I am an implementing consultant. While here, we'll implement those procedures that apply to you that will allow you to get more done in less time. This program is designed to improve your personal productivity.

"John, to really improve your personal productivity, we must cover three areas. I view them as part of a circle and inside the circle are three parts.

"The three parts in the circle are: your paper managing, e-mail and telephone habits; your management techniques; and how to manage yourself. All three parts are covered when I work with people."

"The best way to increase your productivity is to:

1. Increase your level of concentration.

2. Reduce the distractions which come
   from the two P's: people and paper."

John agreed that this approach made sense to him.

I then said, "Most people can not manage paperwork as efficiently when their desk is cluttered with paper."

"The secret to learning how to manage from a clean work area is knowing the five action decisions on what to do with the paperwork!" I said.

John asked, "Should I be taking notes?"

I replied, "I would because we'll be covering a lot of information."

"When you pick up a document, regardless whether it's one page or ten pages, you only need to read one or two paragraphs to know what to do with the paperwork. You'll then choose from five action decisions on what to do with the paperwork. Does this approach make sense?"

John nodded.

"Now tell me, John, do you know what those five action decisions might be?"

John thought for a few seconds and said, "Throw the paper away."

"Right," I said, "But you can also shred or recycle. This action decision is very important, because many people have never learned to throw things away. If you don't think you will need the document, then throw it away. A good rule of thumb to use is, 'the originator usually keeps a copy.' The more files you keep, the longer it takes to find a file. E-mail is a great place to keep files so long as your e-mails are kept in sub-folders.

"One individual I worked with had saved copies of his last fourteen years of expense reports. It took me over an hour to convince him that it was okay to throw away all but the previous 12 months. After we threw away his old expense reports, he could then start throwing away the other old files."

I then asked what the second action decision might be on what to do with the paper.

John thought for a few seconds and said, "You can give it to someone else."

"Right," I said. "You can delegate it to another person. Now, how about a third action decision?"

"File it," John said.

"Very good," I replied. "You can file it away for future reference."

"And if we're not going to throw it away, delegate it or file it, what else can we do with the paperwork?" I asked. "And before you answer, 'put it on your desk' is not one of the five action decisions, that is an indecision."

John laughed and said, "It's starting to get more difficult."

"Don't overlook the obvious," I said.

John thought for several seconds, then said, "Take immediate action."

"Right," I answered. "So what is number five?"

After almost a minute, John said, "I don't know!"

"John," I asked, "What do you do with a document that you need take action on, but not immediately?"

He replied, "I put it in a stack, write a note on my calendar and get to it later."

"How well does this system work?" I asked.

"Well," he responded, "Sometimes I forget to write it on my calendar; the item gets covered up in the stack, and as a result, I don't get it done on time."

I asked, "What kind of calendar do you use?"

"I use an executive planner," said John.

"When you open up the calendar what does it show: one-week, two-weeks or a month?" I asked.

He replied, "It shows one month. It works pretty well, but I often find I don't have enough room to write all the information I need. What kind of calendar do you use?"

"I use an executive planner that shows only two weeks at a time," I said. "I find it gives me enough room to write the information I need. Because I do most of my work at the client's office, I must always have my planner with me."

I continued, "Does Joyce schedule meetings for you and, if so, how does she do it?"

"Yes, she does schedule my meetings and she uses the same type of calendar I use," he said. "However, keeping the information the same on both calendars is a problem."

"Trying to keep two paper calendars the same is 'an impossible dream' and will always be." I said. "Because it can't be done. I understand you have e-mail?"

"Yes, we do."

"Do you use Microsoft Outlook?" I asked.

"Yes, we do. Why?" he asked.

"Because Microsoft Outlook software has an excellent electronic calendar," I said. "I recommend that, when software is available, the executive and his assistant use the same electronic calendar, rather than two paper calendars. It's simply a matter of printing out a copy of the calendar once a day.

"This allows the person to have a copy of the calendar to take to meetings. All electronic calendars have limited space, so abbreviate when you can. For example, if you're having a meeting with someone, you don't need the word 'meeting' in the calendar."

> *When printing the monthly calendar, click on page setup, then select "don't print weekends." By eliminating printing weekends, more information is shown on the calendar. You may also want to print the next five weeks, instead of just printing one month.*
>
> *Make sure you allow for unscheduled items. One client had two bosses, his primary boss and one with dotted line responsibility. Each boss would take about four hours of his time each week. However, he didn't know when they would require his time. I advised him*

to allow for this every week in his calendar.

"Also," I continued, "your calendar must be realistic. For example, if your boss consistently takes more time than is scheduled in his staff meeting, don't schedule any activities immediately following his meetings.

"I find many people are downloading their computer calendars on electronic devices. Some people use these devices instead of paper. You can also buy a cellular telephone with a similar device built-in.

"Finally," I said, "the fifth action decision you can make with a piece of paper is follow-up. This fifth action decision is critical to learning how to handle paperwork effectively!"

The five action decisions on what to do with paperwork are:

1. **Destroy, throw away, shred or recycle.**

2. **Delegate or route the paperwork to someone else.**

3. **File. Put the paperwork in a file for reference later.**

4. **Take immediate action. This means you need to take care of this item now.**

5. **Follow-up. When you need to take action or follow-up on an item but not now, schedule the**

item by putting it in a follow-up file.

There are three types of follow-up files.

1. **1-31**. This file contains thirty-one partitions representing the maximum number of days in any month. You can use an accordion type file, or if your desk allows it, you can make your own follow-up file using hanging folders, my preference. Using thirty-one small tabs (1/5"-Cut) work best. Put the tabs on the front of the hanging folders, staggering the tabs so you can see each one.

2. **January through December.** This file contains twelve partitions, one labeled for each month in the year. This file supplements the 1-31 file and is used by those people who have many follow-ups several months out. The first of each month, pull those items out for that specific month and put them in the follow-up file according to day. When using the 1-31 follow-up file, if you indicate the month and day for follow-up on the document, you don't need to use a January through December follow-up file.

3. **Monday through Friday (M-F).** For those that do not need to follow-up beyond a week, set up a M-F follow-up file. I've found that many customer service people find a M-F follow-up more practical since they must respond to their customers in a short period of time.

Set up either a 1-31 or a M-F follow-up file,
don't set up both.

Illustration of a 1-31 follow-up file:

The follow-up files are used for two functions:

1. Scheduling your work.
2. Following-up on delegated items.

"John," I said, "When you use a follow-up file, schedule your paperwork using your calendar. Learn to plan your workload by scheduling projects on those days you need to work on them. For example, if Monday is the twentieth of the month and you want to work on this item on Wednesday, then put the item in partition number 22. If you have an item you need to work on Thursday, then simply place the document in partition number 23."

"Who should maintain my follow-up file?" John asked.

I replied, "That is a good question. It depends on the individual. I recommend when you first start using the follow-up system that you maintain it yourself. After a few weeks you may want Joyce to take over your follow-up file.

When someone else maintains your follow-up file, you must indicate on the document, when the item is scheduled for follow-up. Write the follow-up date in the same place on each document. By the way, Joyce should also use a follow-up file."

> *One very important technique that I learned*
> *as a manager is that you should always fol-*
> *low-up on most items you delegate.*

I then asked, "John, what reputation do you have in your organization regarding delegation? Do you never follow-up, sometimes follow-up or always follow-up?"

John looked at me sheepishly and said, "Never."

I continued, "Several years ago I took over a sales division from a manager who seldom followed-up. All of his people knew this, and when he asked them to do something they didn't want to do, they simply didn't do it. Two months after I began, all my employees knew that I followed-up on everything! Remember, the manager who has the reputation of always following-up has more efficient employees."

He said, "I'm starting to understand how important managing paperwork is to supervising people."

A follow-up file is a critical management tool.

I said, "Before we go further, let's discuss the importance of e-mail and how it fits into the paper managing program. Would you agree that e-mail is no different than paper mail, except for the method of transmission?"

He agreed.

I then said, "If we agree that there is no difference between paper mail and e-mail, then the same five action decisions should be used, right?"

John thought a few seconds and said "That's right."

Let's review the five action decisions we learned when managing paper, and see how they fit when processing e-mail.

1. **Destroy.** There is really no difference between destroying paper mail and destroying e-mail. Simply delete the item.

2. **Delegate.** You can delegate e-mail about the same way as you would paper, just add your comments, then forward it to the person involved.

3. **File.** To file an e-mail, it's a simple matter of setting up an electronic file folder in which to file the e-mail for reference. Make sure that the names on your folders make sense, so you can find the

information when you need it.

4. **Take Action.** Taking action on an e-mail is some-times more complicated, especially if you need to consult with other people. I recommend, you print all *action* items.

5. **Follow-up.** Following up on e-mail is more diffi-cult. There are three ways to follow-up on e-mail.

   a.   Print out the e-mail and put the paper in your 1-31 follow-up file as previously illustrated.

   b.   Send an e-mail to yourself for receipt at a later date. Microsoft outlook also has a task section that allows you to follow-up on items electronically.

   c.   Set up your own electronic follow-up file (EFF). First, set up an electronic folder, called follow-up, under whatever area you want. Then, set up thirty-one sub-folders (1-31) under the follow-up folder. Note: You must prefix the single digit numbers with 0, such as 01,02,03. Setting up this file will take less than 10 minutes.

        You'll find that using the EFF for following-up on e-mails is very easy. After you've sent your e-mail, go to the sent file, click on the e-mail you want to follow-up, drag it to your EFF and put in the appropriate day."

For those of you who have many old e-mails in your electronic in-basket, I'll bet you are using it for following-up. I suggest you use one of three ways described to follow-up on e-mail action items.

"John," I said. "We've now covered the concepts on how to be more efficient at managing paper and e-mail. Will these ideas work for you?"

John nodded his head, smiled and said, "Yes, and I now understand why you said earlier that you cannot handle each piece of paper only one time. If you make one of the five action decisions with a piece of paper, and that decision is to follow-up, then you must handle that piece of paper again."

"You're exactly right!" I replied. "Our next step is to learn the types of paperwork, their location and what files you need to set up."

CHAPTER 3

Types of Paperwork and Location of Files

I LOOKED AT MY WATCH. I'd been in John's office for about an hour, and we had covered quite a bit of material. John's desk was still covered with paperwork, so our next objective was to clear off his desk and keep it clear.

I said, "One very important aspect of good paper handling is being able to locate those files when you need them. Do you find that, sometimes, when you're in your office, you can't find certain files?"

"Absolutely," John replied, "There are times when I'm working on a project or someone will call me about something, and I can't find the item I need. It just about drives me crazy. I hope you have some ideas on how to locate files faster."

I continued, "Being able to locate files when you need them is very much a part of the paper managing program. Remember *'Cardinal Rule No. 1'*: All your files should be in hanging file folders so they can be filed vertically, and you can find them quickly. Before we start clearing off the top of your work area, I want to explain to you the three types of files."

"Three types of files?" John said, as he started taking notes, "I thought there was only one type of file."

> *When I'm working with a client who starts writing, I quit talking. If I keep talking while they're writing, one of two things will happen. First, they probably won't hear what I'm saying. Second, if they quit writing, they'll probably forget to write down what they wanted to remember.*
>
> *When I am conducting workshops and I see my audience start writing, I will repeat what I had said a few times, before continuing.*

I explained there are three types of files that you use in your office:

1. **Reference Files.** These are the most common type of files. They contain information that requires no further action. An example of a reference file would be a paid vendor file. This file contains copies of all the invoices for a particular vendor that have been paid and require no further action. Another example of a reference file would be previously processed and paid expense reports.

2. **Working Files.** Working files are those files that contain information that requires further action. The follow-up file is a working file in that it contains

material that requires further action at a later date. Another example would be the current budget file you're in the process of finalizing. Another would be a project you're currently working on.

3. **Reading File**. This file contains reading material such as magazines, technical journals, etc. This file is not used for company reports. I suggest that you have an area in your office designated for your reading material.

I continued, "We've covered the different types of files, along with a brief description of each. There is one other important part of paper handling. Frequency of use should be the primary factor as to where files should be located."

John thought for a moment and said, "You're right, how frequently you use the file should determine the location."

I said, "John, I see that your desk has two deep drawers, one on each side of the desk, and both drawers are set up for hanging file folders. Are both drawers full?"

John pulled out both drawers, looked in and said, "Yes, they are."

I said, "Would you agree that, of all the places in your office, the two drawers in your desk are the most convenient locations for vertical files?"

John thought for a moment and said, "You're probably right. I never thought of it that way before, but locating frequently used files in those locations would be appropriate."

I then said, "I see both drawers are currently full of files. What files do you have in those drawers?"

"I'm not sure," he said. "I very seldom use those files."

I continued, "Are you telling me that you're not sure what is currently in the most convenient locations in your office for files?"

"You really know how to embarrass someone!" he said. "That's right, I'm sitting here at a desk covered with paper, and the most important space in my office are full of files that I don't use."

I replied, "Please, don't be embarrassed, because this is very common. Would you like to know an easy way to clear out the files on both sides of the desk?"

Of course, he did.

I then said, "Ask yourself these two questions:

1. Do I use this file frequently, (daily or weekly)?

2. Do I need quick access to this file?

If the answer is no to both questions, then the file belongs somewhere else."

For the next several minutes John started removing files

from both desk drawers. We were able to determine what classifications they were and what action to take on them. For the files we were uncertain as to the importance, we left them on the floor.

After we applied these two principles to the files in his desk, there was only one file left: his budget file.

> *For most of you reading this book, if you have a work area with limited drawer space, this space will be full. If you will apply the two principles on what you should do with these files, 80% to 90% of these files will go some place else. Many will be trashed. This clearing-out process is vital to implementing the paper handling program.*

I continued, "Sometimes, there is a third factor you might consider for which files should be in your desk drawer. If your desk is the only location in your office you can lock, you may want to include some confidential files in your desk drawer."

> *Most people have little time to clear out their area during regular office hours. I would encourage you to take time during off-hours to clear out your work area. For this program to work, you must have the file space to set up appropriate files.*

"John, what is that basket on top of your desk, piled high with paper?" I asked.

"That is my in-basket," John replied.

"That is the worst place you could have it. What happens when someone puts something your in-basket?" I asked.

"I usually stop what I am doing and see what came in." John replied.

I said, "I have found that very few crises come via paper. Unless you are looking for something, I would ignore new mail until the end of the day."

I continued, "An in-basket on your desk is very distracting. You may want to keep your in-basket on your credenza behind you. You also might have your mail go directly to Joyce. She can then bring it to you once or twice a day."

I asked, "Do you have a mail slot?"

"I sure do," John replied.

I said, "You may also want to leave your mail in your mail slot until you are ready to handle it. Some people hang an in-basket on the wall outside their work area. Take your pick, but let's remove the in-basket from your desk!"

John decided to put his in-basket behind him on his credenza and have Joyce bring in his mail.

The telephone rang. John looked at it and saw who was calling. "This is the boss," he said. "I should answer this call."

I replied, "I'll take a quick break, and after the break we will begin the process of having you clear off the top of your desk, one item at a time."

"Sounds fine to me," John said as he turned to answer the telephone.

During the break, I walked around and looked at the work areas of his direct reports. As I suspected, most of the areas were similar to John's: desks piled high with file folders and loose papers. The offices were also very cluttered. While in the Air Force, I was taught the meaning of leadership. And that is to establish the work ethic which your employees will mimic ... good or bad! John had unintentionally established the office standard for his employees, a cluttered work area.

CHAPTER 4

How to Clear the Paper Off the Top of
Your Work Area and Keep It Clean

AFTER THE BREAK, I said, "John, we've now covered the fundamentals of how to manage paper and e-mail. Is there anything we've discussed that you don't understand?"

John replied, "No, I have a good understanding of the principles, and I'm ready to start implementing them."

I said, "When we were clearing out your desk drawers, I noticed that you've have some stacks of paper on your credenza. We want to clear off those stacks as well.

"The purpose of this exercise is for you to learn how to make a decision about each piece of paper, so that you will no longer stack paper on top of your work area."

I continued, "I believe that the most difficult thing about the clearing-off process is learning to make one of the five action decisions about your paperwork."

"During this process you must accept this fact: there is a

proper location for each piece of paper in your office. The top of the desk is not one of them unless you are working on the item."

"Now, before we start, what are the five action decisions we can make on what to do with paperwork?"

John thought for few seconds, then replied, "Destroy it, file it, delegate it, take action, or follow-up."

"Exactly right," I said. "During our break, I made up a follow-up file for your desk. Using thirty-one hanging file folders, with a small tab (1/5"-Cut) on the front of each folder. I staggered the tabs so that each is visible."

"Since you'll be using this follow-up file frequently, which side of your desk would be most convenient for you?" I asked.

John replied, "Probably the right side."

I asked, "I noticed that your hanging files face away from you and not toward you. Would it be more convenient if they faced you?"

"It certainly would, but how can you do that?" he asked.

Most desks that allow for hanging files have a partition built into each drawer which enables you change the direction the files face. Check your desk drawers for partitions.

John was fortunate as both drawers had partitions. We

moved each partition to the middle of each drawer so that the hanging files now faced John.

I then put the follow-up file in the right side drawer, so it was facing John.

"I didn't know you could do that" John said. "With my files facing me, it'll certainly make finding them much easier."

"John," I asked, "Are you ready to start the clearing-off process?"

"Yes," he replied. "I am."

"The process starts by picking up a document from the top of your desk. You must make one of the five action decisions, and you cannot put the paper back down on top of the desk. There is one very important thing you must do during the clearing-off process: you should schedule your paperwork in conjunction with your calendar's activities."

For those that have never used a follow-up file, you may need to change your thinking about planning your paperwork. Because you have not been scheduling your paperwork but have been reacting to paperwork, it may take you 30 to 60 days to learn how to comfortably schedule your paperwork.

If you are in the sales field, following-up is critical to being successful. Use these files to follow-up on such things as prospects and customer orders.

John picked up a piece of paper, looked at it and said "I don't need this anymore," and threw it away.

The next piece of paper belonged in a working file that he had stacked on top of his desk. "Do you remember what the three types of files are?" I asked.

"Yes," John replied. "Working, reference and reading files."

"That is exactly right," I said. "Now, what type of file do you have in your hand?"

"This file is part of a project I am currently working on, so it'd be a working file," he said.

"Would it make sense for you to use the right side of your desk for your current working files?" I asked.

"Certainly," he said. "I have a tendency not to keep all the information together in my project folders, and as a result, I'm always looking for something."

I continued, "The drawers on the left side of your desk can be used for those reference files which you need quick access to."

I labeled a hanging file folder with the project name and handed it to John. John took the file folder, put the documents for that project in the working file and filed it in the drawer on the right side of the desk.

"Now, about the documents that you just put in a project file and filed away, will you need to take any further action on the project?" I asked.

"I sure will," he said. "In fact, I need to work on it next week."

"John," I said, "You just filed away a project that you need to work on next week. How will you remember to work on it?"

John got a very puzzled look on his face and said, "The project file is too large to put in the follow-up section. What should I do?"

I answered, "Make yourself a note or take a document out of the project file which would remind you to work on the project and place that document in the follow-up file. You can also use OUTLOOK TASKS feature and indicate start and due dates electronically."

> *When I work with lawyers, CPA'S and clients who have large working files, those files should be stored in a working file area. Use a document to schedule the project in the follow-up file.*
>
> *Use a check list for each client, indicating what needs to be done, along with a completion date and put this list in the follow-up file. Some clients like to have two copies of the check list, one for the follow-up file and one for the working file.*

"John, the process we are going through now is vital to the success of this program. It is absolutely essential, as we go through the clearing off the desk process, that all appropriate files be set up at that time."

The next item John picked up was something that he needed to take action on, but not immediately.

"John," I said. "You indicated that this item is something you must do yourself, but not immediately. What are you going to do with it?"

He replied, "What I typically do is put it in a to-do stack and write a note on my calendar."

I asked, "Now that you're using this new system, what are you going to do with this item?"

"I'm going to put it in my follow-up file for next week," John replied.

"That's right," I said. "You can schedule it in your follow-up file for any day next week."

> *When scheduling paperwork, you should check your calendar first before you put an item in follow-up. By using a follow-up file to schedule your workload you can make sure you are not overloading certain days.*
>
> *Some people schedule time on their calendar to handle their paperwork.*

The next item John picked up was some paperwork that needed to be put in a reference file.

"John, will you need quick access to this information?" I asked.

"No," he said. "This is information I may never use, but then again, I might need it someday."

"In this situation, designate an area either in your work area or in a filing cabinet outside your work area for this type of infrequently used reference files," I told him.

"Sounds fine to me," he replied. "Joyce has a filing cabinet in her work area that would be a perfect location for this file."

Over the next several minutes, as John picked up each piece of paper, he decided what he should do with the paperwork. I helped by labeling hanging file folders so the files could be set up. This process is the only way I know to effectively clear off the top of a work area. You must learn to make one of the five action decisions with paperwork and not put it down on top of your work area. This change of habit is the most difficult part of the process!

Some people use file folders, label them and put them inside hanging files.

John picked up some paperwork that he needed to talk to his boss about.

"What do I do with this item? I want to talk to my boss about it, but it's not urgent," he asked me.

"There are three additional working files that we need to set up. These are boss, employee and peer working files.

"What is your boss's name?"

"Bill," he said.

"Let's set up a hanging file with Bill's name on it; and file it in front of your follow-up file. This folder can be used for you to accumulate information that is not urgent, but for which you need to talk to your boss about. Remember, the information that you put in this working file does not require immediate action."

I then asked, "I believe you told me earlier that you have six direct reports, is that right?"

"Yes, including Joyce," he answered.

I asked, "What are the other names?"

He replied, "Mary, Bob, Megan, Rich and Rose."

I said, "Let's set up a working file for each of your direct reports. Since Joyce is right outside your office, we probably don't need a working file for her."

> *For those of you that have an assistant, schedule time each day or week to meet with them.*

We then set up the working files for each of his other direct reports and placed them behind Bill's file. Many people use different colored plastic tabs for these files. We staggered the tabs, so the names could easily be seen.

> *It is a good idea to meet at least once each week with your direct reports. Some managers schedule time each week, while others schedule the time when needed.*

I asked, "Do you have any peers that you work with regularly?"

"Yes," he said. "I work very closely with two product managers, Don and Charlie."

I said, "Let's set up files for Don and Charlie and put them behind your employee working files. Are you starting to understand how we're going to use these working files?"

He replied. "I believe so. We're going to use these files to accumulate non-urgent items for discussion later. These files will work great for me. I have a habit of laying on my desk paperwork that I want to talk to my boss, employee, or peer about, then forgetting to follow up because it's buried."

"Do you remember early in our discussions when I talked about increasing you productivity by increasing your level of concentration?" I asked.

"I sure do," John replied.

I continued, "Do you also remember me mentioning that, to increase your concentration, you must decrease your distractions?"

"Yes, I remember that, too," he said.

I went on to say, "Distractions come from the two P's: people and paper. Have all your direct reports set up a working file for you. Insist that they accumulate non-urgent items in your file which will reduce your distractions."

John stood up with a surprised look on his face and said, "At least 10 to 15 people pop-in on me every day with non-urgent issues. In fact, it has just now dawned on me that I'm a pop-in myself!"

I continued, "Where do you think your people learned to pop-in? John, don't feel like you're the only manager that has experienced this problem. There are thousands of managers doing the same thing and wondering why they have so many interruptions.

"What would you do if you had a non-urgent document that needed to be sent to someone in your office? How would you get the document to that person?"

John thought for a few seconds and then said, "I would probably take the document to the person myself."

"So, you would just pop-in?" I asked.

"Yes," he said. "But isn't that taking action now?"

"You're right. But, there is another way you can do it."

"How?"

I replied, "You can set up an out-basket in your office to accumulate non-urgent items. When you're ready to leave your office, you can take several items at once. Instead of delivering the item directly to the person, I would simply put the item in their mail slot. You can also delegate emptying the out-basket to Joyce."

John leaned back in his chair and said, "I've been encouraging these distractions myself!"

"I have two statements I'd like you to learn," I said. "One I created. And the other I read in a book. The one I coined goes like this: 'The absence of criticism is implied approval.' The second one is, 'What we allow, we teach.'"

John replied, "I understand what you're saying. I have been promoting this pop-in behavior."

"The boss is usually the one who establishes the behavior in the office. What do you think is going on throughout your organization?" I asked.

John replied, "Everyone is popping in on everyone else, and I am encouraging the practice. I have a question. I have heard many managers say they have an open door policy, but how does this apply to pop-ins?"

I replied, "My definition of an open door policy is if the

item that you need to see me about is urgent, I will see you as soon as I can. However, if the item is not urgent, put the item in your working file for me and set up an appointment to see me later."

I asked, "John do you have staff meetings?"

"Yes, I have a weekly staff meeting with my direct reports," he answered.

"If you have an issue that comes up during the week and is important enough to talk to your staff about, what do you do?"

John thought for a moment and said, "I put the item on my desk, along with all of those other items I want to discuss at the next staff meeting. Many times, the items get covered up, and, then I forget to discuss them at the staff meeting."

I said, "You should set up a staff meeting working file in your desk and accumulate those items you want to discuss at the next meeting."

"Good idea," he said. "But I'd need to set up two files: one for my team meeting and the other for my boss's staff meeting."

We then set up files for both meetings.

"John," I said, "I think you will find setting up working files for most activities will save you time."

John replied, "You're right. These files will save me a lot of time searching for items. I'm starting to understand this whole process more clearly. By setting up vertical hanging files, properly labeled, for all the projects in which I'm involved, I'll be able to find what I need much faster."

I then said, "When you have all your direct reports on this program, they will interrupt you less. When you implement this process throughout your organization, the productivity for most of your people will increase. Did you notice, however, that I said most people?"

"Yes, I did," he said. "Are you saying not everyone is going to participate?"

I replied, "The program I am outlining to you will work only for those who make it work. There are some people who have a very difficult time operating from a clean desk and resist change. There are some employees who have their own systems, and, if it works for them, that's fine.

"I've made it my policy to never work with anyone who feels they don't need help. Over the years, I've had a few situations where someone did not want me there, and the program never worked. You can't help anyone until they want to be helped."

There was a knock on John's door.

"John," a voice said. "I need to see you about something important. It will only take a minute."

Standing at the door was Bob Jennings, one of John's direct reports.

"Come in, Bob. I'd like you to meet Maynard Rolston. He's a management consultant, and he's showing me how to get more work done in less time!" John said.

Bob and I shook hands, then Bob turned to John. "Sorry for the interruption, but I have this problem and need your advice."

Bob explained the problem. After much discussion, John gave Bob his opinion on what to do. Bob apologized for the interruption and left the office. I noted that the interruption took about eight minutes of John's time.

I turned to John and said, "Not only did you just have a pop-in, but you also took his problem in the process."

John replied, "You are exactly right, Bob did pop-in, and I did take his problem. This same thing has been happening to me for years."

"Was the problem urgent?"

"Not really," he answered.

I reminded him, "What we allow, we teach."

John nodded his head in agreement.

I continued, "Now, I want you, one item at a time, to clear off the top of your desk and your credenza. Then, after lunch, I want to cover some other things that will save time. Also, don't forget the files you put on the floor.

"John, when you put an item in follow-up that will take a considerable amount of time, schedule time on your calendar to do it, just like setting up a meeting."

The next item John picked up, he indicated that he needed to take action himself. I then asked, "John, could someone else take care of this item?"

John replied, "Megan could."

"Then why don't you delegate this issue to Megan?" I asked.

John got a surprised look on his face, wrote a note on the document asking Megan to take care of this item, along with a desired completion date, and put it in his out-basket.

> *It's up to you when to put an item in a person's working file or send it directly to them. If you want the person to start working on the issue immediately, I would send it to them and not put it in their working file.*

For the next two hours, John and I cleared all the papers. During this process, we set up several working and reference files and also filled three waste paper baskets. He also scheduled two projects on his calendar and put several items in his follow-up file. He used the drawers on the left side of his desk for quick access reference files. These included his budget, previous expense reports, computer reports, organizational charts, notes from previous staff meetings and lists of telephone numbers.

He also had two more pop-ins and took three telephone calls.

One file that is very useful to set up is an instruction file. This file can be used to hold instructions for your equipment, such as voice mail, e-mail and computer codes. This file also works well at home.

What you will find when you go through this process is that most of the paper does not require any action, but usually requires a file to be set up or thrown away.

I asked John to apply the same action decisions to his e-mail. I encourage people to clear the paper off the desk first to help them learn the discipline of making the action decisions. After you have learned these habits, clearing out e-mail is fairly simple. I suggest e-mail action items be printed, so that the paper follow-up file can be used to schedule all action items.

Remember "Cardinal Rule No. 2": All action items, regardless of source, should be in paper form.

"John, are you having fewer pop-ins this morning than you usually do?" I asked.

"Yes," he replied. "I'm having far fewer people coming into my office."

"Why is that?" I asked.

"Probably because you're sitting in my office," John answered.

"Why can't this be normal?" I asked him. "If your people had an urgent matter to see you about, my sitting in your office should not discourage them."

John got a surprised look on his face and said. "You're right, if they had an urgent matter to see me about, they would have come into my office regardless."

I asked, "Do you use an attache or brief case?"

John replied, "Yes I do, why?"

"I see one under your credenza, does it contain any paperwork?"

John reached under the credenza and placed the attache case on top of his desk. He then opened the case, and we found it contained a large amount of paperwork.

I asked, "Do you take it home with you every night?"

John thought for a second and said, "Yes, I do take it with me almost every night, but I seldom open it when I get home."

"John," I said. "Quit taking the case home with you, and instead start scheduling the work in your follow-up file.

"Okay now, empty the contents of the case on top of your desk."

After John emptied the contents, I said, "Now, using the five action decisions, please clear the contents off the top of your desk."

John started clearing everything using those five action decisions. A few minutes later, the desk was cleared.

> *Write notes on the back of the documents with which you are working. That way, your notes are never separated and, should you need to copy the document later, it is not defaced.*

I continued, "There may be occasions when you must take work home, but I discourage it. I believe you should keep the office separate from your home. However, if you're working on a big project, and no one is home, then staying home to work on it makes perfectly good sense.

"John, you have done a great job learning how to manage paper and e-mail. Let's take a lunch break, and after lunch we'll discuss some techniques that will improve your telephone skills."

CHAPTER 5

How to Use the Telephone Effectively

"JOHN, WE HAVE talked about paper and e-mail managing techniques," I said. "Now, let's discuss how to use the telephone effectively. Before we continue, I want to ask you this question: if you need to respond to someone, how would you go about it, go see the person, use e-mail, or leave a voice mail?"

John thought for a while and said, "Before I met you, I would have gotten up, walked across the hall and popped in. Now, I would probably send an e-mail."

I then said. "The fastest way to respond to someone is to use the telephone. There is a reason why the telephone is faster, do you know why?"

John replied, "I'm not sure, why?"

"Most of us can talk *seven to ten times faster* than we can type or write. Anytime you can, use the telephone as it is the fastest way to communicate. The only real disadvantage to using the telephone is lack of documentation. In the future, computers will be able to translate your voice into data. This method will give you the speed of voice mail and the documentation of e-mail."

Here are five tips for effectively using the telephone:

1. **Leaving messages.** When you leave messages on voice mail, include as much information as practical so the person you called can do what you want done without having to call you back. Make sure that you leave your name and telephone number along with your message. This method also works if you are leaving a message with a person, and not voice mail.

2. **Calling someone.** When you call someone, the first thing you should do is to identify yourself. I am amazed how many times people will call other people, and just start talking without identifying themselves. After you have identified yourself, you should then tell why you are calling. Within a few seconds, both parties will know who is calling and what the call is about.

    The third thing you should do is ask the party you have called if this a convenient time to talk. I am astounded how many people answer the telephone while having a meeting in their office. If you don't ask this question and just start talking, the person in the meeting won't be listening to what you're saying.

3. **Setting up appointments.** Setting up meetings

with individuals can be a very frustrating situation. When I call to set up an appointment, I'll give the person's assistant, or leave a voice mail message, at least four different dates I would be available to meet. If possible, make sure that the four different times cover a two-week time span.

4. **Setting up a time to talk to someone.** There are times when voice mail communication will just not get the job done. If this is the case, you must communicate directly with the individual.

   The method I use is to talk to the person's assistant to obtain times the person would be available for a telephone call. Be sure you get more than one time the person will be available. I note this information on my calendar for follow-up.

   If the person with whom you are trying to talk does not have an assistant, then leave a message on their voice mail asking what times they will be available.

5. **Your voice mail message.** Voice mail, when properly used, can save you hours on the telephone. Make sure that the message on your voice mail is kept up to date. If you're going to be out of the office a few days, or even a day, make sure that your voice mail message informs the caller when you will be gone and when you will return.

   You may want to program your telephone so that all your calls go directly to voice mail, without the telephone ringing three times.

It's also a good idea to leave another person's name and telephone number that they can call if they need to speak to someone.

I once called a person three or four times in a week and left messages. After my last call, I finally talked with someone and was told the person I was trying to reach was on vacation.

"John, have you noticed that at no time have I suggested that you ask the person you are calling how they are doing?" I asked.

"Yes, I have," John said. "Are you encouraging me to be unfriendly?"

I replied, "I'm certainly not asking you to be unsociable, but if you want to spend less time on the telephone, don't ask the person how they are doing. It will just extend the conversation. Of course, if there is a company philosophy regarding asking how people are, you should continue to do so."

"John," I asked, "how do you now handle your voice mail messages?"

John replied, "When I return to my office, I play each message, stop after each message, write down the caller's name and phone number and why they are calling. I then use the list to return my calls. After I complete each call, I scratch the name off my list."

I said, "If you're using a recorder, that is about the only way to do it." I said. "However, if you're using voice mail, I think there is a more efficient way. Do you remember the five action decisions on what to do with paperwork?"

"I do," John replied. "Trash, delegate, file, take action now, or follow-up."

"Exactly," I said. "Now, I want you to use the same five action decisions on voice mail. Remember, you should make only one of the five action decisions for each piece of paper you pick up, don't lay the paper back down on your desk. Making a list for each phone call is like putting the paper back down on top of your desk. I suggest, after each message, you make one of the five action decisions with each message. Most voice mail software allows you to pause, key in a code, and respond to the message. Most also allow you to send the message to someone else.

"I've observed people handling voice mail for years, and have found that making one of the five action decisions after each message is the most efficient way to handle voice mail. If you're not ready to take action now, write down the action item and schedule it in the follow-up file. You may want to respond to the person, to tell them it will take you some time to do what they want done."

Sometimes, when you are short of time, you will need to play all messages first, to determine if there are any urgent messages.

"Using this method eliminates numerous telephone lists. Will this method will work for you?" I asked.

John agreed, saying, "I believe this method should eliminate some of the problems I have in using a list. I put the message on a list, but I don't have a method of making sure I respond to every telephone call. I think this idea will help me."

"When should I answer my telephone?" John asked.

"That is a great question," I replied. "I think that depends on what is going on in your office. If you are having a meeting or working on an important project, do not answer the telephone. Have Joyce answer it and, if it is urgent, she will let you know. Caller ID is a great device to have on your telephone."

"That is very good advice, thanks," John said.

I continued, "Another telephone technique I use is to write down all the items I want to discuss with the person I am calling before I make the call. I list them in the order of importance. If I don't do this, I may overlook an important item."

> *This is the same technique I use when seeing a doctor. I write down everything I want to discuss with the doctor before I go to the office. I also take a pen and note pad with me, so that I can make notes on what the doctor tells me.*

"Do you ever have a caller that you just can't seem to get off the telephone?" I asked.

John replied, "Yes, all the time. Do you have ideas that will help?"

"I sure do," I said. "Since the caller can't see what you're doing or who is in your office, simply pretend someone just came in your office for a meeting or that you have a meeting to go to. I have even known people to ring their own doorbell at home or knock on their own office door to get people off the telephone.

"I had a client who talked on the telephone too long. This person was very outgoing and liked to visit. After making her aware of this problem, I suggested a way that would help reduce her time on the phone: Before you make each call, jot down how long the call should take. After each call, write down next to the expected time exactly how long the call took. Do that for all your calls for a few days. After that, total the time you expected to spend on the call and the time you actually spent on the call. By comparing these totals, you'll find out if you're a telephone culprit.

"After using this procedure, she discovered she was losing almost five hours a week talking on the phone too long. Once she became aware of this problem, she was able to significantly reduce the time she spent on the telephone."

I continued, "Another client, who was a vice president of a large medical association, hated e-mail. He was the type of person who would rather talk about something than write about it. I asked him why he didn't answer some of his e-mail using voice mail. He got a strange look on his face and said he didn't think that was possible. Once he started replying to appropriate e-mails by voice mail, his personal productivity skyrocketed."

> *Don't hesitate to use the telephone instead of e-mail. Just because someone sent you an e-mail doesn't mean you can't answer by voice mail. Remember, because voice mail is the fastest way to communicate; you can talk seven to ten times faster than you can type or write.*

"John, remember always look for the fastest way to do things. If documentation is required, you might have to write a letter or send an e-mail.

"The experts tell me that over 80% of the telephone calls are not returned. I think that is a frightfully high percentage. I believe that you should return all telephone calls. Remember, you can delegate the returning of phone calls."

John replied, "I have never considered having someone return some of my telephone calls. But now that I think about it, it sure makes sense. Thanks for the tip."

"Now, we're ready to learn the other two parts of the circle, starting with how to delegate effectively."

CHAPTER 6

How to Delegate Effectively and Improve Employee Productivity

I CONTINUED, "John, you have learned that there are five action decisions on what to do with paper, e-mail and the telephone. Which decision do you think is the most powerful: take action now, delegate, file, trash or follow-up?"

He thought for a few seconds and said, "I would think taking action."

I replied, "I am convinced that delegating is the most powerful. It involves more than one person, and I find most managers are not very good at delegating. In your case, because you have six people reporting to you, delegation is six times more powerful than taking action."

"I never thought of delegation that way before," he said.

"A few years ago, I spent some time with an individual who had worked for his company for over 15 years. The last five years he had been working over 70 hours a week. He was a family man with two children. He admitted that, over the last several years, he had slighted his family in favor of his job. This individual had five direct reports, and had a total of about 75 employees.

"I spent the first few hours working with him, explaining the paper managing program; setting up a follow-up file, working files and reference files; and throwing away a lot of paper. When we got to discussing delegation, I asked him if any of his direct reports were working the same number of hours as him?"

He looked out the window and very sheepishly said, "No."

This man had eliminated the most powerful decision of all, delegation. He was trying to do everything himself. It took me over two hours to convince him he had competent people working for him and that he should start delegating. When he finally started delegating, he worked fewer hours and his department accomplished much more work.

"John," I said, "The best definition of management I've ever heard is 'getting things done through people.' I believe you'll never be an outstanding manager until you learn how to delegate effectively."

To this day, I still don't know why so many managers resist delegating. I believe most managers simply don't know how to delegate effectively.

> *Why is not delegating effectively one of the most common problems in business management today? Because it's not taught in school, and there is a lack of good management training in most companies today.*

"John," I continued, "After working with many managers, I've learned five reasons why most managers are hesitant about delegating."

1. **Fear:** Many managers are afraid that employees will not do the task right. Ask yourself, if they make a mistake, what is the worst thing that could happen? Most of us learn more from our mistakes than from our successes. Make sure you don't delegate a job to someone you know can't handle it.

   There is a certain amount of risk when you delegate, but you must take that risk. If the employee is not trainable, you have little choice but to replace them. You cannot do their work for them!

2. **Quality:** Many managers feel their employees cannot do the task as well as they can do it. Many very smart people fall into this trap.

   Most people improve the quality of their work the more times they do it.

3. **Time:** Another common perception is the feeling that it will take too long to explain to employees

how to do the task. Managers believe that doing it themselves is easier than explaining how to do it to the employee.

If you take time to explain how to do the task, it will more than pay off in the long run.

4. **Concern:** Many managers feel sorry for the staff and feel they are working too hard. Take a look at the hours your staff is working compared to the hours you are working. The key word here is working. Remember EPI!

5. **Qualifications**: Finally, many managers are concerned the employee is not qualified to do the job. If this is the case, you have three choices: give the project to another employee, train the employee to handle it or replace the employee. A manager who ignores this situation will bury themselves in work, and many times, will lose their job as a manager. Remember, an important part of your job as a manager is to ensure that your employees are well trained.

"John," I said, "I once worked with a manager who worked 45 to 50 hours per week, and took 30 to 35 hours of work home. This manager had nine people working for her.

"After determining how much work could be delegated, she came to the realization that she could delegate four hours of work each week to each of seven people, two hours of work per week to one other person and six hours of work per week to another. In all, there were 36 hours of work per week she could delegate.

"She implemented the program, quit taking work home and her people are getting more done. Also, none of the nine employees spend any more time in the office than before."

> *I recommend you maintain a business relationship with your employees. I have known managers who became friends with their employees, and it affected how they evaluated and managed their people. As a manager, you must not lose your objectivity when evaluating employees. It is difficult to give a friend a poor performance rating.*

"John, there are three questions I have managers ask themselves to find out if they're delegating enough."

1. Do your employees seldom work overtime?
2. Do you work late nights, and, sometimes, take work home?
3. Do you fail to allow time in your schedule for planning?

"If you answered yes to any of the three questions, you are probably not delegating enough."

"Wow," John said, "I answered yes to all three questions!"

"Does Joyce ever work overtime?" I asked.

"Never," John replied.

"Well, you're probably not delegating enough to her." I said.

He replied, "You're right. I have this very competent employee right outside my office, and I'm not giving her enough to do."

I continued, "Do you realize your assistant can actually get much more work done than you because she has far fewer interruptions than you?"

If you're the one who is delegated to, please understand that I'm not talking about dumping so much work on people that they can't get their job done. I've learned over the years that most people like to be challenged and busy.

"John," I asked, "Do you screen all of your e-mails?"

"I do, and it's a major use of my time. People are sending me e-mails I shouldn't be getting, and I'm spending hours viewing e-mails," he said.

I continued, "Have you ever considered having Joyce screen your e-mail and take action on those items she can handle? Also, have you had her contact those people that are sending you e-mails you don't want, telling them to stop sending them to you?"

"No. I haven't," he said.

"Why?" I asked.

"I've never thought of it," he replied.

> *If you are getting e-mails you should not be receiving, do something about it! Let those people know that are sending you these e-mails to stop sending them to you.*

"Most managers never even come close to delegating enough items to their assistants and end up spending many hours in their offices doing things they should have delegated. John, I want you to start thinking of all the activities you can delegate."

I continued, "John, a few years ago, I was having lunch with my consulting mentor, and we were discussing delegating. He felt many managers were fearful about delegating to their employees because they might make mistakes. He advised using a three-step process:"

1. Have the employee bring you an issue with their recommendation, review it with them, and let them do it.

2. After about a month, have them bring to you the issue after they have made their decision.

3. After another month, discuss the issue with the employee after they made the decision and implemented it. This process works well, because it trains managers on how to delegate, and also eliminates any big disasters."

"That is some great advice on delegating," John said. "I'm going to implement his suggestions.

> *As a manager, you should make sure that your employees are working on worthwhile activities. Ensure your employees are adding value to the system and not just expense. In other words, are you spending more money on the activity than it is worth?*

"John," I said. "Because of the cost of employees today, managers cannot allow them to do tasks that don't make economic sense. One example is to have all employee expense reports checked, and have changes made regardless of the amount, does not make economic sense."

> *When you delegate always explain why and how it should be done. I believe people should know why they are being asked to do something.*

I explained to John that delegation can go different directions:

1. Downward — Boss to employee.
2. Upward — Employee to boss.
3. Laterally — Peer to peer.

I continued, "Now, let's talk about downward delegation. This is the most common type and there are some important principles that managers should follow. If there ever was a cardinal rule in delegation, it would be:

*Never delegate any item without designating
a realistic completion date.*

"I find this is absent most of the time when managers delegate. Make sure you and your employee agree that the completion date is realistic."

*As an employee, make sure that items
delegated to you have realistic due dates. I've
never known a manager who delegated items
to his people knowing they could not complete
them on the due date.*

I said, "Most urgent issues don't start out as urgent issues. When employees are given tasks with unrealistic completion dates, you're doing nothing more than scheduling problems. When this happens, employees are quite creative in coming up with reasons why they could not get the task done on time."

*Remember, if your boss gives you a task with
an unrealistic due date and you don't say
anything, guess what your boss is assuming?*

"Another form of delegation is upward delegation, which happens frequently. Many experts advise managers to never allow an employee to bring them a problem without having a solution to the problem. I don't agree with this advice. If an employee brings you a problem and doesn't offer a solution, it's difficult to give that problem back to the employee.

"I suggest you use the word recommendation instead of

solution. Using recommendation allows you to hand the problem back to the employee and ask them what they think should be done."

> *For those of you who occasionally bring a problem to your manager, without having a recommendation and he or she takes it, you're losing valuable training in problem solving.*

"John, have you ever asked yourself when you should be required to make a decision for your people?" I asked.

John thought for a moment, and asked, "No. I never have, why are you asking?"

"Many years ago," I said, "I read in a company manual an excellent definition as to when a management decision should be required. The explanation given was, 'A management decision is required when all the information available does not make the decision evident.'

"If someone brings you a problem to handle and all the information available indicates what should be done, why should that person be bringing you the problem? The exception might be if the decision is above his or her level of authority."

John replied, "That is a great definition, I will remember that in the future."

"John, there is another area in which you should be careful, that is accepting problems in meetings. Do you ever leave meetings with you being responsible for most of the action items?" I asked.

"You really have my attention this time. This always happens to me. What am I doing wrong?" John asked.

"My guess is that you are answering your own questions," I replied. "After you state the problem, do you usually give the group your idea for a solution?"

"I do it all the time!" he said.

I then said, "Try this approach: after you've stated the problem, issue, or opportunity, ask the group for their opinion on what should be done. I call this technique 'bottom up communication.' Gaining consensus by assuring everyone is allowed to give their opinion on issues helps develop a good management team."

John leaned forward, put both hands on his desk and said, "No wonder I'm working long hours. I've been taking on too many problems in my own meetings."

I continued, "One word of caution .... don't allow the most vocal people in your group to comment first. If you do, they may influence the opinions of the other people in the meeting."

John then said, "That is a great idea, this technique will allow me to get comments from all my people before I state my opinion. This should result in more unbiased comments from all my employees."

"Using this technique," I said, "You'll also be amazed at the comments you'll hear. You'll also find out who your stars are. If you don't use this technique, you might not hear the best answer.

"A few years ago I was working with a president of a small college. He worked very long hours, was not delegating effectively and was taking on too many problems. When discussing taking those problems, I told him that doing so allowed incompetence to hide."

He looked at me in amazement and said, "I've been doing that for years. I don't even know who my best people are!"

I continued, "I once worked with a golf club professional who was working 80 hours a week. He had a wife and two children and was so busy he seldom played golf. It seemed like every telephone call was for him, until he realized that most of the calls were for information and not necessarily for him personally.

"He learned the magic of delegation and using a follow-up file. He taught his staff to answer the telephone with, 'Jeff is busy right now, may I help you?' He now works fewer hours, his staff's efficiency improved, he plays much more golf and has more time with his family.

"John," I said, "Peer-to-peer is simply lateral delegation, and all too often the one who is the best talker doesn't take on the problem.

"There is another rule in delegation: always follow-up.

"Next, let's discuss ways that you can help employees improve their productivity. The proper equipment can do wonders in helping people get more done. Many managers mistakenly think equipment that can improve employee productivity is an expense, rather than an asset."

"John," I asked, "May I use your white (chalk) board?"

"Sure," he replied.

I then drew a chart on John's white board.

Equipment cost as compared to people cost

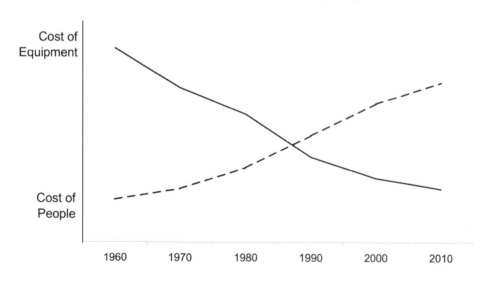

"John, this chart illustrates how equipment cost in comparison to employee cost has changed. The chart also shows, how over the last several years, employee cost has risen and equipment cost compared to the cost of people has decreased.

"The reason I started the chart with the year 1960 is because that was the year the first transistorized computers were installed. These computers were light years ahead of the old tube computers. Compared to the computers of today, they are antiques. In 1960, computers cost about a million dollars each. That same year, people who had good jobs, made about $3.00 per hour or about $6,200 per year.

"Today, however, you can buy a computer with over 30 megabytes of memory along with a hard disk that stores millions of characters, for a about a thousand dollars or less. No wonder thousands of employees have their own computers.

"John, as you can see on the chart, equipment cost in relationship to people cost switched in the mid-80s. Today, you should be spending company dollars on equipment that will improve your employees' productivity."

The largest expenses on most company profit and loss statements are employee salaries.

"Take, for example, the photocopier. To save on the number of photocopy machines, some managers will buy one expensive photocopier and locate it at one end of the building. Over the next several months, thousands of dollars in employee productivity will be lost from people walking back and forth to a remotely located photocopier."

I then asked, "Do you know what else happens when you create a situation like this?"

John replied, "What?"

"Because the employees are gathered around the machine, waiting for each other to finish copying, they will have photocopy meetings."

"You're right," John said. "I've seen that several times as I walked by the photocopy area."

"The number and location of photocopying equipment should be determined by usage, not by number of people." I said.

"The same logic also exists in how many fax machines or computer printers are installed in offices. You should determine the number required by usage, not by number of people"

John replied, "I am embarrassed; I've been making some of my equipment purchasing decisions based on early 70s' thinking."

"John," I said, "Many managers are still making equipment buying decisions based on 70s' economics. One of the easiest ways to increase company profit is to improve employee productivity not by slashing head count."

"Do your employees work on special projects?" I went on to ask.

"Of course," John replied, "We work on many such projects throughout the year. Why?"

"Do you require those appropriate projects to have written schedules prepared?" I asked.

John thought for a moment and said, "No, I don't believe we require any written project schedules."

"Are most of your projects completed on time?" I asked.

"You must be a mind reader because we seldom complete our projects on time. Do you have any ideas that will help?" John asked.

"Many years ago, when I was in the computer business, IBM personnel taught me that you should prepare written schedules for most projects. Are you familiar with written project schedules?"

John replied, "Well, are you referring to a schedule that shows a start date followed by all the steps necessary to complete the project? Each step has the estimated time required along with the completion date."

I replied, "That's exactly right. Some people also call them Gant charts. Why don't you require them on your special projects?"

John said, "Because I was assured that this process was not needed. It sounds like I need to review this policy."

"I once worked for a manager whose department required no written project schedules. When I asked why the projects were not getting done on time, I was told that 'management kept changing the rules.' After the manager required all appropriate projects to have written project schedules, more projects were completed on time.

"Microsoft office software has a program called Microsoft Project. It's a fine program for helping people prepare project schedules. There are two very important things about using written project schedules. First, you can determine before the project begins if it can be completed on time. Second, by reviewing each schedule, managers can ensure that the employees have considered all the processes and that the time schedule is realistic. It's also a great tool for managers to use for following-up on projects."

For those of you that are doing projects, learn more about how to better manage your projects. It will make doing them easier.

John said, "I am going to spend more money on buying equipment and software that will help my employees work more efficiently. I realize how everything you've covered so far ties together."

I said, "Remember, your people will make you successful, so let them! Next, let's discuss the ways you can reduce the time you spend in meetings."

CHAPTER 7

How to Spend Less Time in Meetings

"JOHN, do you attend a lot of meetings each week?" I asked.

"It seems like all I do is attend meetings," he replied.

I then said, "Let's discuss some ideas that will decrease the number of meetings you attend. As a director, you are high enough in this organization that this technique should work for you.

"Never commit to a meeting unless you are furnished an agenda prior to the meeting. Of course, if your boss or a customer invites you to a meeting, it is hard to insist on an agenda, but you can still ask for one. Otherwise, you simply don't agree to go to the meeting."

"Won't that make people mad at me?" he asked.

"I doubt it," I replied. "Asking for an agenda before the meeting is not unreasonable. Now, stop and think. When someone invites you to a meeting, shouldn't that person have some idea of the subjects that will be discussed?"

John thought for a moment and said, "You're right. I never have a meeting without first preparing an agenda."

I know a Vice President that insists he also be furnished the desired outcome of the meeting and what the person wants, is it a decision or information only.

I told John that receiving an agenda before the meeting will allow him to make one of three decisions:

1. I am going to attend the meeting.
2. I am not going to attend the meeting.
3. I am going to send someone else in my place.

I continued, "After implementing this policy you'll be amazed at how fewer meetings you'll attend. You will also notice that the meetings you are attending will be better organized because you insisted on an agenda.

"John, do me a favor, look on last month's calendar and count the number of meetings you would not have attended had you received an agenda before going."

John located last month's calendar and began counting. After few minutes, he said, "I probably would not have attended eight meetings."

I said, "Now, total the number of hours you spent in those eight meetings you shouldn't have attended."

John went back and counted the number, coming to a total of 12 hours.

"If that is typical, you're spending 144 hours per year in meetings you shouldn't be attending. This amounts to three and a half weeks per year."

John looked amazed and said, "From now on, unless I'm invited by my boss or a customer, I'll insist on an agenda before I commit to attending any meetings."

Don't schedule your activities too close or too soon. If you're flying in late in the afternoon or evening, don't schedule meetings early the next morning, especially in the winter time, where flights are often delayed!

I then shared with John the principles that I follow regarding meetings:

1. Each meeting should have an agenda. Which should clearly outline the purpose of the meeting along with what subjects will be discussed. The agenda or a memo should specify the time and length of the meeting.

   Regardless of your title, I would ask for an agenda before you commit to attend a meeting. You may want to see if a company policy could be established requiring meeting agendas.

2. All meetings should start on time.

    *If there are 12 people in the meeting and the
    meeting starts 10 minutes late, 2 hours of
    productivity was lost.*

3. All meetings should end on time.

4. Notes should be published following the meeting,
    outlining the subjects covered along with all action
    items. For each action item, the person responsible
    and the completion date should be shown.

    *Exactly who is responsible for taking notes
    is often an issue. You might rotate the
    responsibility among the staff.*

    *After taking notes in meetings, people have
    a tendency to put their notes aside and forget
    to schedule their action items.*

    *Take 3 X 5 cards to each meeting, note on
    separate cards the action items you received.
    Use these cards to follow-up.*

"John," I continued, "For meetings to end on time, someone
must be managing the meeting. To manage a meeting properly,
you must first create an agenda and determine how long each
subject should take. Do you remember what we talked about
regarding project scheduling?"

"I certainly do," John replied, "You must establish a start

date and a completion date, determine the steps required, and decide how long each step should take. A completion date must then be assigned for each item."

"Exactly right," I said. "You must manage meetings the same way. Break down the subjects that are to be discussed and assign an allotted time for each one. During the meeting you must make sure that each subject is covered in the time allowed."

John asked what happens if someone exceeds their allotted time.

"That is where managing the meeting comes in. Depending on the subject, you may have the person curtail their discussion and defer it to another time. The important thing is that you must maintain control of the meeting or it will not finish on time.

"While working at a client's office, I was asked to make sure his next day's meeting would end on time. I asked for the agenda and found that the meeting was scheduled for two hours and had 24 items on the agenda. My client asked me to be the 25th item, and wanted me to comment on my observations.

"The first thing I asked my client was which items were most important. I then allocated time for each subject, allowing for extra time, until I had used all two hours. I entered on the agenda the time when we should be on that item. For example, I estimated we should be on item six at 2:30 p.m. I then managed the meeting by time periods. When the meeting started, my client introduced me and said I was responsible for assuring the meeting ended on time."

I continued, "By using this technique, the meeting did, in fact, end on time."

John asked, "Did you have to ask anyone to quit talking?"

"Yes, I did," I replied.

"Did anyone get angry?" John asked.

I replied, "A couple of people were a little upset, but for the most part people complied with the schedule. I did let each person know how much time they had before they spoke.

"You must consider the money that is being wasted when meetings are not run properly. If there are several people in the meeting, you could be wasting thousands of dollars in people's time."

"I never considered the cost involved," John replied.

"Does Joyce schedule your meetings?" I asked.

"Yes," John replied, "she schedules most of my meetings."

"For how long do you usually schedule your meetings?" I asked.

"Usually for about an hour," he said.

I said, "I suggest you begin scheduling most of your meetings for 45 minutes. I've found that if you allow one hour, the person is going to take an entire hour. How many one hour meetings did you have last month?"

John picked up last month's calendar and counted, "I had 32 one-hour meetings last month."

"John," I asked, "How many of those could have been 45 minutes?"

John started counting again, and after a few minutes said, 25 could have been 45 minute meetings.

I continued, "If you multiply 25 by 15 you get 375 minutes, or over six hours you would not have been in meetings. That's almost two weeks a year."

John stood up with a very disgusted look on his face and said, "I took only one week of my vacation last year, because I had too much work to do. I now realize I'm spending over five weeks a year going to inappropriate meetings and spending too much time in the meetings I do have!"

I then said, "Don't feel alone, you've fallen into the same trap as many managers do. You have not been managing your own activities. By the way, did your direct reports take all of their vacations last year?"

John looked straight at me without smiling and said, "I don't want to answer that question."

"You just did, John." I said.

"Do you have any occasions where people take more time in meetings with you than you had scheduled?" I went on to ask.

John replied, "I'll guess over half of the meetings I have in my office don't end on time. Is that my fault?"

"I believe it is," I said. "Here's a tip I have used for years that usually gets meetings to end on time. I call it the ten-minute warning."

I continued, "When you start the meeting, confirm with the people, how long the meeting is scheduled for. When there are only ten minutes left before the meeting is to end, you let everyone know. Many meetings don't end on time because when the meeting is scheduled to end, some important issues have not been discussed. Does this sound familiar?"

John responded, "It sure does, and the meeting drags on and on."

I then asked, "Do you receive many reports?"

He said, "Several every month and some contain 20 to 30 pages."

"Do you need most of the information you get on these reports?" I asked.

"As a matter of fact, I have to scan through several pages

just to get the information I want," he responded.

I continued, "Have you ever asked anyone to condense or summarize the reports you are receiving?"

John didn't realized he could have these reports modified in such a way.

"John," I said, "you have a very responsible position in this company, and your time is valuable. I spent 10 years in the computer business, and learned many reports prepared on a computer can be changed. Are most of the reports you are getting prepared by the people who work for you?"

"Yes," he replied.

"I would outline exactly how you want your reports prepared. If you had your reports prepared the way you want them, how much time would you save each month reviewing them?"

John thought for about a minute and said, "About three hours a month."

"That's about one week a year. Have the reports changed," I said.

"Before we leave the subject of reports, I want to caution you about spreadsheet reports. These reports appear to have been prepared by a computer, but many times the information shown has been manually prepared. One of my clients was receiving a 15-page report every month, and it was taking his staff 25 hours each month to prepare. When he discovered how much time was required, he reduced the size of the report and saved his staff over 15 hours each month."

> *If you or your staff are spending several hours a month preparing reports, inform the people receiving these reports exactly how many hours are involved in preparing them.*

John said, "I'm surprised at how a few minutes' savings on several items can add up to such large amounts of time. You just showed me how to find six weeks a year. I'm truly amazed!"

I then said, "We're now ready to discuss some ideas that will show you how to improve your self-management skills. Let's take a short break; you can check your e-mail and voice mail, and I want to check my own voice mail."

CHAPTER 8

How to Better Manage Yourself

I SUMMARIZED, "We have now covered the first two parts of the circle: the fundamentals of managing paper, e-mail, the telephone and management techniques. The third part of the circle is how to manage yourself more effectively.

"I believe you have more control over your time than anyone else," I said. "Would you agree?"

John looked at me and said, "I've never thought of my time that way, but yes, I do."

I then asked, "Have you ever heard of the word oxymoron?"

"I sure have," John said, "I believe it means a figure of speech that has a contradiction of terms, such as cruel kindness or to make haste slowly."

"Exactly," I said. "Have you ever heard the term time management used?"

"I hear that all the time," John said.

I then said, "I think the term time management is an oxymoron. If you think about it, no one can manage time. Time goes on whether we like it or not and we all have the same amount of it. However, you can manage yourself.

"Do you remember in our previous discussions, I said that helping you get more done in less time was a three-part program?" I asked.

"Yes," John replied, nodding his head, "I certainly do remember. You said that handling paper, e-mail and the telephone were the first part and management techniques was the second part.

"I have learned a great deal from you on how to be more efficient, especially in delegation, following-up, not taking on problems and reducing meeting time."

I then said, "The third part of the program is how to better manage yourself. Of these three parts, which do you think has the greatest influence on how much work you get done?"

John thought for a minute and said, "I'd guess my management techniques have the most influence on my productivity."

I said, "I think it's a close race between management techniques and managing yourself. I've found one's ability to effectively manage one's self has the greatest impact on individual productivity. Stop and think: I could be an excellent manager and a world class paper manager, but if I didn't manage myself wisely, I wouldn't get much done."

Image

"John," I said. "There are two good reasons for being better organized. First, you will get more done in less time and second your image will improve.

"People with very cluttered work areas are sometimes perceived to be not very organized and consequently not very efficient. I have known of employees not being promoted because of the appearance of their desks"

I then said, "There are two sayings about one's image: 'You are not what you are but what you are perceived to be,' and 'perception is reality.'

"I once worked with a partner of a very large law firm. The firm hired only the top law school graduates. While I was in his office, we talked about image and how it could adversely affect your career. He then told me an interesting story. He said, one day a wealthy couple were in his office. While there, they asked if his firm had a good tax attorney. He told them the firm had some excellent tax attorneys and set up an appointment for them to meet with one of the firm's best.

"A few weeks later, while at a social function, he again met the couple. He asked them how they liked the attorney that he had recommended. 'Oh', they said, 'his desk was so cluttered we felt he would misplace our tax problem and forget to work on it, so we went elsewhere.' "

I then said, "John, in this situation, perception was indeed reality."

John asked, "I wonder if my cluttered desk has affected my not being promoted to vice president."

I replied, "That, along with your personal productivity could have had an influence. Now that you are better organized and have a different image, we'll see what happens in the future."

If you have a very cluttered work area you might find out if the appearance of your work area is adversely affecting your career.

Your Worth Per Hour

I said, "Before we continue, John how much are you worth an hour?"

John gave me a puzzled look and said, "No one has ever asked me that before, I have no idea what I'm worth an hour. I don't even think I know what I make an hour!"

I continued, "If you divide your annual income by 2,080 hours, you'll get your hourly rate. Because you have company benefits, such as health, life insurance and retirement, you'll need to add about 25% to your hourly rate to find out what you're getting paid. Remember, I didn't ask you what you're paid an hour, I asked you what you're worth an hour."

John took about a minute to figure his hourly rate of pay. After he finished, he looked at me and said, "Now I know what

I'm being paid per hour. Does this figure have any bearing on how much I'm worth per hour?" he asked.

"Not really," I said. "But you should be worth more than you're getting paid. Your worth per hour is an excellent gauge to use before getting involved in certain business activities.

"I developed this approach after working with several lawyers. Since I am from a family of lawyers, one thing I know about most of them is that they are poor delegators. I suspect this trait goes back to law school when professors required everyone to research their own cases.

"Many years ago, while working with an experienced attorney whose desk was piled high with paper, I asked him what his billable rate was."

"One hundred seventy-five dollars per hour," he replied.

I then asked him if all the issues on top of his desk were worth $175 per hour.

He paused for what seemed like five minutes and said, "No, they're not."

"Then, why are they on top of your desk?" I asked.

Many lawyers are very pragmatic people, and need a good reason to change their behavior. By using a billable rate per hour ($175) as a benchmark, they find that it is easy to determine which issues need to be delegated.

"When my client began comparing the values of the issues on top of his desk to his billable rate, he delegated much more work to both the paralegal staff and the legal secretaries. His personal work load decreased and his annual income increased.

"I've been using this worth-per-hour technique for years. It's a great gauge to help most people determine what business activities in which they should be involved."

> *Regardless of where you are on the organization ladder, you should determine your own worth per hour. It is a great method to help you choose your business activities.*

I then asked John if he was comfortable with $400 per hour for his worth.

John thought that it was too high.

I asked, "What about $300 per hour?"

He paused for a few seconds, then said, "That's a great deal of money, but, considering what I am responsible for, that might be about right."

> *Most managers grossly underestimate their worth per hour. This results in their involvement in business activities that should be delegated to their staff. There is a direct correlation between what managers feel they are worth per hour and how much work they delegate.*

I asked, "Do you remember before you scheduled items in your follow-up file, you checked your calendar to ensure you had the time available to do them?"

John replied, "Yes."

I said, "Looking back, how many of the items in your follow-up file should you have delegated, based on your time being worth $300 per hour?"

He replied fairly quickly, "I would have delegated many more items. I'm starting to see how many activities I've been involved in which I shouldn't have been. I take it, that's what my direct reports are for?"

Schedule Time on Your Calendar

"You're exactly right," I said. "Do you remember talking about how, when scheduling an item in follow-up that takes a lot of time (one or two hours), you should schedule it on your calendar, just like a meeting?"

"I certainly do," John said. "And that tip should really help me. Before, I never scheduled work on my calendar, and I found I never had time to do my own work. As a result, I either took work home or stayed late at night. Should I schedule time on my calendar to do my work?"

"That technique works for many people," I replied. "If you can make it work for you, start blocking out time on your calendar."

Anticipate delays. Don't try to schedule your activities too closely to each other. If your meetings are in different locations, anticipate traffic problems when scheduling. Show up early for most meetings and have other work you can do while waiting. Remember, you can't make up time! If you're late, you're late. Being consistently late is one of the worst habits you can have.

Office Meetings

"Now that you're a member of the clean desk club," I continued, "I want to share a tip that will make meetings in your office more productive. When you have a meeting in your office, clear off the top of your desk. When I first met with you, your desk was piled high with paper, and you lost eye contact with me several times during our discussion."

"That certainly is poor body language," John replied.

"Yes," I said. "And you also probably didn't hear all of the things I said to you. If you clear your desk, your attention level will soar, and your office meetings will be more productive."

I have never known anyone who could, from behind a cluttered desk, maintain their concentration while having a conversation with anyone on the other side of their desk!

Presentations

"Do you make presentations to your bosses, and, as a result, find your ideas either approved or disapproved?" I asked.

"Several times a year," John said.

I asked him if he most often won or lost.

"I win about 60% of the time, but would like to know how I can raise my percentage."

I said, "Many years ago, I worked for the most organized man I ever knew. Many of the techniques I use today I learned from him. One method he had perfected was how to get his programs approved by upper management. I call this technique selling the program prior to the meeting.

"Before the presentation, make separate appointments with each of the people who will be judging your presentation. It is important that they understand that you will not be asking for their approval but for their opinions. Using this approach, you will hear most, if not all, of the objections that each has on your presentation. Many times these people will caution you about other members' hot buttons. After you have met with each one, modify your presentation according to what they told you."

John thought this idea made perfect sense and said, "Sometimes, I've been surprised during my presentations with an objection I had not considered. Great idea! I'll start using this method immediately."

Strategic and Operational Activities

I said, "I believe executive activities are divided into two distinct categories: strategic and operational. Strategic activities are directed toward the planning processes such as deciding what areas must be considered now for success in the future. Operational activities are the day-to-day actions taken in your area of responsibility.

"As you go higher in an organization, the more you should decrease the time spent on operational activities and increase the time for strategic issues. What percentage of your time do you think you spend on strategic issues?" I asked.

After about a minute, John said, "I spend about 10% of my time on strategic issues and 90% on operational issues."

"Now, what percentage do you think you should be spending on each of those two subjects?" I asked.

He thought some more and said, "I should probably be spending at least 50% to 60% of my time strategically, and the rest operationally."

I said, "Most of the executives I work with do not allow enough time for strategic activities. By better managing yourself, you'll be able to spend more time on strategic issues."

Problem Solving

I continued, "Before we finish this part of the program, I want to share with you the method I use to solve problems.

Problem solving is a three-step process.

1. You must identify the problem, not the symptom. If an employee is frequently late, for example, that is not the problem, but the symptom. You must first identify what is causing the employee to be late.

2. After you have identified the problem, develop a solution or solutions that will solve the problem. I learned years ago, from my business mentor, that there is usually more than one way to solve a problem.

3. Select the best solution and ensure that it is successfully implemented."

"That is an excellent approach to problem solving, I will use it in the future." John said.

Summary

"Before we go to the next subject," I said, "Let's review the options you have to better manage yourself:

1. Manage from a clean desk. This will decrease your distractions, increase your concentration and improve your productivity.

2. Use a follow-up file to schedule your paperwork, giving you more control over your work load. Also, follow-up on most everything you delegate.

3. Keep in mind your worth per hour and delegate more work to your direct reports. Stop taking so many problems from your staff. Also make sure that your direct reports are delegating all appropriate work to their staff.

4. Use your boss, employee and peer working files to accumulate information and reduce pop-ins. Ensure that all your direct reports follow the same practice.

5. Delegate more to Joyce, including the screening of your e-mail. You also may want to have your mail sorted. A good method is to use is colored folders, one folder for signature items, one for action items and another for correspondence. Have the reading material put directly in the reading file.

   Ask Joyce to prepare two more stacks. One stack will represent the paper that you should not even be receiving while the second stack will contain those issues Joyce feels she can handle herself. The key is that she determines what goes in each stack. Then, simply review each stack with Joyce and make any necessary adjustments. After a few weeks, those two stacks will disappear, and you'll receive much less paperwork.

6. Require an agenda before you agree to attend a meeting. Change meeting duration when appropriate from one hour to 45 minutes. Also, remember to give a 10-minute warning before the end of the meeting.

7. Require formal project schedules when appropriate. This will reduce the time you take finding out why the projects were late.

8. Have reports you receive reformatted and reduced in size to decrease the time you spend searching for the information you need. I know a vice president who has his assistant highlight all the important items on his reports before he receives them.

9. Improve your employees' productivity by requiring all the appropriate items we have covered to be implemented throughout your organization.

10. Spend more time on strategic issues and less time on operational activities. Remember, strategic issues should be handled by you and not delegated.

11. Always do what you said you were going to do, when you said you were going to do it. Develop this habit and you will be more successful."

Even though many of you reading this book are not directors, you can use many of these options to improve your self-management skills.

I then asked, "John, do you now realize how much control you have over your activities?"

"I am speechless," he said. "I never realized I had all these options available to me. I've been blaming other people for my long hours."

"When we first talked," I said, "You told me you were working 70 hours a week and estimated you were getting about 35 hours of work done. When you implement the items that we have discussed that you feel appropriate, what effect will this have on the number of hours a week you're working?"

After a very long pause, John stood up, shook my hand and said, "I should reduce the amount of time I'm working by 15 to 20 hours a week and get more work done in the process. I'm also going to spend more time on strategic planning. However, the most important thing I'll get from this program is that I'll have more quality time for my family and myself."

CHAPTER 9

How to Plan for Tomorrow the Night Before

"WE HAVE SPENT most of the day together, and we've discussed many issues. Now, I want to cover how you plan for tomorrow the night before." I said.

"I'm very interested in hearing what you have to say, because I've never planned for my next day's activities." John replied.

I continued, "I suggest you start this process about 30 minutes before you leave the office for three reasons. You can stay late, take work home, or come in early the next day. If you wait until the next morning to plan the day, you lose those three options. I'm not endorsing any one of those options over the others, but merely saying that planning the night before has three advantages.

"Planning the next business day is a three-step process.

"Step one is to handle new paper mail, e-mail and voice mail. Use only four of the five action decisions with each document. Do not take any action. If you start taking action, you will not leave the office on time."

"For each document, you must decide whether to trash, file, delegate, or follow-up. If you need to take action the next business day, leave those documents on top of your desk temporarily. Continue making those decisions until your new mail is handled. One word of caution: taking action on e-mail is sometimes very difficult. I recommend e-mail action items be printed and included in the paper process.

"Sometimes you will have items left over which you didn't get done during the day. Put those items with the new mail action items on top of the desk. We will get to these items later.

"Remove the items scheduled for the next business day from your follow-up file and put them on top of your desk. If Joyce is maintaining your follow-up file, have her bring you those items before she leaves.

"In the real world, you must prioritize your work twice. Once when you first put the item in follow-up, and second when you remove it from follow-up while you are planning for the next business day.

"Step two is to spread out all the items that are on top of your desk so you can see each one. This will include follow-up items, new mail action items and items not completed that day. I believe it's difficult for most people to look at an item by itself and determine if it's the most important issue.

"It is, however, quite easy to compare all the items on top of your desk to each other and prioritize them in the order in which to handle.

"After you determine which item is first, turn it face down on top of your desk. Then determine which one is number two and place that item face down on top of number one. Continue this process until all the items on top of the desk are face down in one stack.

"Step three is to turn the stack of papers face up. The items are now in order of priority. Next, check your calendar to see if you can get all these items done the next business day. If you feel you can, put the items back in the follow-up file and go home.

"If you believe you cannot get all these items done the next day, then you should check the item on the bottom of the stack to see if it really needs to be done the following day. If not, reschedule it in follow-up. Keep checking the items from bottom up to verify if they need to be done the next day. Do this until you feel you can get the remaining items completed.

"If you still feel all the items need to be done the next day, and you don't think you can get them all done, you should delegate some of the items.

"If you still feel, after going through this process, that you can't get all the items done, then you can stay late, take work home, or come in early the next business day. However, it's very important, that before you leave the office, you know that you can get all the items scheduled done the next day."

I then asked John to go through the three-step planning process, which took him about 15 minutes. After he completed the process, I asked him what he thought of the planning-for-tomorrow process.

"I am absolutely amazed!" he replied. "I've never prioritized my work so fast. I prioritized 15 items in less than a minute."

I said, "After you've prioritized your next day's work, place the items in your follow-up file or in a desk drawer. When you're ready to take action on them, take one item out at a time and work on it until it's finished.

"By setting up priorities daily, you work only on the most important items first. When someone brings you an item, you can easily determine if it's more important than the one on which you are working. If it is, put the current issue aside and handle the higher priority item. If it is not, then keep working on your number one issue and schedule the other item for later. This approach ensures that you'll always be working on the most important item."

> *When you learn to prioritize your work it also makes the decision on when to answer the telephone much easier.*

"This solves one of my biggest problems," John said. "And that is going back and forth between items during the day. It is also great to plan tomorrow the night before. This is something I've been missing for years. It should help me with my planning. Thank you!"

"Congratulations," I said, "You have now learned how to manage from a clean desk! Do you have any questions?

John responded, "Yes, I do. What do I do about the notes I have taken?"

"Good question," I said. "Put your notes in your follow-up file for a week from now. Review your notes each week for the next few weeks, then put them in your personal file. Some people type up the five action decisions on 3 X 5 card and put the card on the wall next to their computer or a prominent place as a reminder."

For those who travel, pay close attention to your travel schedule. Don't try to schedule things too closely. Also don't schedule yourself out of the office on consecutive weeks. You must have time to do your office work!

I continued, "Before we finish this part, I want to cover the steps you should take after have been gone a week. You do take vacations, don't you?"

A huge smile appeared on John's face, and he said, "I'm going to be taking all my vacations from now on."

"Great," I laughed, "The last thing you should do before going on a vacation is to change your voice mail to give the name and phone number of the person who is in charge while you're gone. You also may want to program your telephone, so that your calls will go directly to voice mail, without the telephone ringing three times.

"Also, leave the same message on your e-mail system.

"While you're on vacation, have Joyce screen and handle all your paper mail and e-mail. On those items that require action, she should send them to the person you put in charge.

"Make sure that you don't load up your calendar on your first day back.

"After your vacation, you should come into the office an hour early. This will allow you to go through your mail without interruptions. You can use the same technique that you used when planning tomorrow-the-night-before. Either file, trash, delegate or follow-up.

"Put the items that you want to take action on that day into a stack on top of your desk. Do not try to take action on anything yet, or you won't get through your stack of mail.

"You should not have any items scheduled for follow-up your first day back. If you did, remove them and put them with the stack of action items on top of your desk.

"Spread out all the items so you can see each one. Set priorities by comparing each item. Follow the same procedure that you used in planning tomorrow-the-night-before by turning each item face down according to priority. Turn the stack of papers face up and place the stack in follow-up or in a desk drawer for processing later. I have found that using a desk drawer works well for keeping the prioritized action items.

"Check your voice mail. There should be no action items on your voice mail because of the message you left. You may want to look at your e-mail, but Joyce should have handled it in your absence."

> *For those that receive many e-mails, you may*
> *want to reserve some time on your calendar*
> *to read the e-mails that came in while you*
> *were on vacation.*

I continued, "Now, you are ready to start handling your action items, one at a time with a clean desk. This is very important. Take one item out at a time and work on it until it is completed or until your priorities change.

"If you put the right person in charge while you were on vacation, you should have few, if any, action items.

"After you have done these processes, you should be ready to take action on those items that require your attention."

> *For those of you who don't have an assis-*
> *tant, ask a fellow employee to help out while*
> *you are on vacation. You can do the same for*
> *them when they're on vacation.*

John replied, "I now realize that I haven't been prioritizing or scheduling my work. I have also been reacting to my paper work as I sort through it."

I stood up, shook John's hand and said, "Congratulations, you've just graduated."

John had a big smile on his face and said, "Thank you so much for spending this time with me. I've never learned more in one day, and it's been a great experience!"

"Before I leave," I said, "I have a question I ask all my clients. Did you get more than, less than, or about what you had hoped for from this session?"

"Oh," John quickly replied, "much more than I expected. I thought you might tell me all the things I've been doing wrong, and leave me with a long list of things I needed to do. Instead, we implemented the program, and I've had a chance to practice while you were with me."

We then shook hands, and I left John's office, saying good-bye to Joyce on my way out.

A week later I called John, who answered, "This is John Jacobs; may I help you?"

"John," I replied, "This is Maynard Rolston, and I'm calling to see how you're doing. Is the desk still clear?"

"The desk is clear, and I love the system!" he said.

"Has your concentration improved?" I asked.

"My concentration has improved tremendously," he replied. "I'm working far fewer hours, and I'm getting much more work done! I must now have this program implemented throughout my entire staff."

"Glad to hear that the program is working well," I said. "I just wanted to follow-up with you, and see how things were going. Have a great day!"

"Thanks for following-up, and I really appreciate your help," John said. "You have improved my quality of life!"

This story is based on my experiences with people for many years. If you will take those ideas that apply to you and implement them, I am confident you will get more done in less time, with less stress, forever!

CHAPTER 10

Making the Process Work
By Don Hutson

WHAT YOU HAVE BEEN READING could have happened in any office, or any company. Our never-ending challenge to be organized and focused is very real. It seems everybody is expected to do more with less. Being better organized can make an incredible difference in your work output, personal performance, peace of mind, and ultimately, your income.

Maynard Rolston's guide to getting more done in less time helps you meet those goals. The challenge is to stay with it, make it a habit, and use the system in a way that maximizes results. Implementing the process is up to you!

This chapter offers ideas on how you can gain maximum benefits from the concepts presented in this book. These concepts work great if you'll make them work. You must incorporate them into your everyday work flow to gain the results you deserve.

The Power of Decisiveness

We must make decisions, live by them, and take action to achieve goals in our lives. We need to proactively make things happen, rather than wonder what's happening.

People have been trying to learn how to make things happen for decades. In the '70s, positive thinking rallies were staged featuring speakers such as Paul Harvey, Norman Vincent Peale, Art Linkletter, Zig Ziglar, and W. Clement Stone. I had an opportunity to be on many of these programs and got to know W. Clement Stone.

One evening, preceding a Chicago rally, the Stones hosted a lovely dinner party in their home in Winnetka, Illinois, for the speakers. Over dinner, I said, "Mr. Stone, you have amassed great wealth and enjoyed a life of much success. To what do you attribute your many achievements?"

I'll never forget his response. He said, "For years, I observed people talking about what they were going to do, but never did. I heard people articulate goals and tasks they planned to achieve, but never did. So many people were never serious enough to get started. The rule that I have lived by for decades is 'Do It Now!' I have placards on my desk at the office and in my study that remind me constantly to 'Do It Now!' I don't procrastinate. I make decisions, put processes in place and work hard for the desired results."

This man amassed enormous wealth with a single yet profound belief that we must have the courage to cast aside any tendency to procrastinate and get started ..."Do It Now!"

That experience had an impact on me. To this day I work diligently not to succumb to the temptation to "Do It Later." I encourage you to embrace this philosophy in terms of your commitment to utilize the ideas in this book to your best advantage. Don't procrastinate, "Do It Now!" Set up your files. Internalize the process.

Develop a Good Reputation for Follow-up

One of the peripheral benefits of being highly organized is that few (if any) items on your task list will fall through the cracks. In the introduction, Chris Crouch, Executive Vice President of U.S. Learning, mentioned the importance of having a good follow-up reputation.

I agree. Years ago, I read that to be a highly credible professional in any field, we should make promises reservedly but always keep them. That is great advice. When we are in the loop on a special project, we will customarily have certain tasks to perform. By accepting the implied responsibilities we have, in essence, made a promise to get something done. Vow not only to keep the promise, but to surprise everyone with your timeliness and your commitment to perform the task excellently. Even simple things like incoming phone messages and how promptly you handle them, impact on your follow-up reputation.

Maynard Rolston's system, as presented in this book, can be one of your first allies for gaining personal excellence, if you vow to use it. I recommend you become self-focused, even selfish, with your system of paper management, organization and follow-up. The most successful people are those who have figured out how to compress more achievement into a given time frame.

The late Heartsill Wilson, a motivational speaker penned the following prose. It puts it all in perspective.

> "This is the beginning of a new day. God has given me this day to use as I will. I can waste it ... or use it for good, but what I do today is important, because I am exchanging a day of my life for it! When tomorrow comes, this day will be gone forever, leaving in its place something I have traded for it. I want it to be gain and not loss; good, not evil; success, and not failure; In order that I shall not regret the price I have paid for it."

Every day is a gift for which we should be thankful. Make the most of it. Plan well, execute with excellence and be proud of your achievements.

The Determination to Prioritize

When I first met Maynard Rolston, over twenty years ago, I was impressed. He immediately came across as an organized, together and knowledgeable individual. I had no idea the impact he would have on me. His influence has been positive on several fronts. I am a better businessman and a more organized professional, but above all, he taught me how to effectively prioritize my tasks and activities.

Prioritizing is one of the critical keys to success. Devoting uninterrupted time to prioritizing, at either the beginning or at the end of the day, is a must for high-achieving individuals. Do yourself a favor and make prioritizing a priority.

One of the greatest benefits of being better organized through this process is that it will free up valuable time to focus on the big picture. Most people do frightfully little long-range planning. You have undoubtedly heard the anecdote that most people spend more time planning their vacation than they do planning their life! Don't let anybody sell you on that plan.

Are you a morning person? An afternoon person? An evening person? Whether it is biorhythms, personal habit, or some unexplainable tendency, there is a time of day when you are at your creative best. This is an excellent time to carve out 15-20 minutes of solitude to think about the big picture in your life. Establish long-range plans, intermediate goals, and, ultimately, daily priorities when you are at your most alert.

The Discipline to Achieve

Discipline weighs ounces and procrastination weighs tons. Vow to internalize the necessary motivation to have discipline. Thoreau defined motivation as "the pull of anticipation and the push of discipline." I have never seen a better definition.

Use your experience and decision-making power wisely. Once your goals and objectives are in place, it will feel good to know that you have a system of prioritizing and organizing that will enable you to enthusiastically attack the challenges ahead.

Confession time! Occasionally, I will get behind on the efficient use of my 1 to 31 and January to December files in my desk. But the good news is that the process works. I can come back into town, go through files, and newly-arrived data, paperwork, etc., prioritize and be back on track within a few minutes.

In conclusion, as good as the ideas in this book are, they are only as good as the action you put forth implementing them. If you are going to operate as a finely tuned achiever, don't disregard the importance of using the system. Staying focused, on-track, and in touch with prioritized tasks will get you where you want to go.

The beauty of this system is that it will reduce anxiety caused by clutter and disorganization enabling you to get more done with fewer distractions. Discipline yourself to use it, profit from it, and you will enjoy peace of mind and a life of greater significance.

Time Management Is An Oxymoron is available at special quantity discounts for sales promotions, premiums, fundraising or educational use.

Call 1/888/888-7696 or write
Leathers Publishing, 4500 College Blvd., Suite 180,
Overland Park, KS 66211
Website: www.leatherspublishing.com

Time Management Is An Oxymoron

The five action decisions:

1. Throw it away.

2. Delegate it.

3. File it for reference.

4. Take action now.

5. Follow-up.